Dear Granny Smith

A Letter From Your Postman

Dear Granny Smith

A Letter From Your Postman

Roy Mayall

First published in 2009 by
Short Books
3A Exmouth House
Pine Street
EC1R 0JH

10 9 8 7 6 5 4 3 2 1

A CIP catalogue record for this book
is available from the British Library.

ISBN 978-1-906021-97-9

For all the old posties who still care.

1

Dear Granny Smith

The world doesn't seem to be made for human beings any more. There doesn't seem to be any room for us. We all have this fantastic new technology: all these computers and mobile phones and Sat Navs and the rest. It's supposed to help us to communicate with one another and to get around the planet without getting lost, but if you ask me no one communicates properly any more, no one gets to know each other, not even their own neighbour, and when it comes to where we are going, the human race is completely lost. No one knows which direction to turn.

I am writing this letter on the day of the national post strike.

I've been on strike a lot lately. There have been many days when the mail didn't come. To be honest, I don't even know if *I* know what it was all about. I mean, I know why I went on strike. I know why I voted for it. But I'm not really sure that the Union had the same set of reasons as me, and I'm not sure, by the time it's all over, whether anything will really have changed.

But I want to tell you why I chose to go on strike.

It wasn't about pay. I'm underpaid. I could do with some more pay. Fortunately I have no responsibilities any more. This isn't true of most of my work mates. Many of them have young families. It's very hard for them, working so hard for so little reward, being so tired at the end of the day that they can't even enjoy their home life properly. But it wasn't about pay for any of us. It was about the future.

It was about the future of public service.

Does that seem like an old-fashioned phrase to you – "public service" – a bit out of place in our modern world?

It's not a term that the managers use any more.

They talk about "products".

That term always puzzles me. What products? We deliver the mail, don't we? We stick letters through letter boxes.

I was talking to one of the guys a few weeks ago. We were chatting about when we had first started out as postmen. He'd been on an induction course over in the main office in the nearby city. This must have been a few years back, since no one goes on induction courses any more. He said they had been asked a particular question by the man running the course.

"What does the Royal Mail deliver?" he had asked.

There were about twenty people in the room. They all had to write down a list.

Letters. Bills. Packages. Postcards. Birthday cards. Magazines. Christmas cards. Presents. Books. DVDs. You name it. I'm sure you could make up a list of your own.

Then the guy running the course went round and asked everyone what was on their list, and everyone read out from their list, and every time someone added a new item, he put it onto his own list on the white board at the end of the room. It got to be a pretty long list in the end.

And then, when everyone was satisfied with the list they had collectively made, the guy said, "But you've missed something out."

Everyone looked at each other then, wondering what it was they had missed out.

"You want to know what you've missed?" he said.

"Yes," they said.

"It's advertising."

See. That's what we deliver the most of. Not letters, or cards or presents. Not bank statements or credit card statements. Not even bills. Advertising. That's what makes up the bulk of the mail. The stuff everyone gets but nobody reads. That's what our "products" are: cheaper and cheaper ways to shovel more and more advertising through your letter box. Stuff you never asked for. Stuff you never needed. Stuff which gets delivered anyway whether you asked for it or not.

Stuff.

We stuff your letter box with stuff. We stuff it through your letter box and then you stuff it into the bin. You say "Get stuffed!" Then the bin men come round and they stuff it into a hole in the ground; or, if you're really lucky, it gets "recycled", which means it gets made into more stuff before it finally gets stuffed into the ground; or sometimes it gets stuffed into a container and delivered to some Third World country, where it gets stuffed into a hole in the ground.

It ends up in the ground in the end.

So you ask me why I went on strike and I could say, "It's so I don't have to deliver quite so much stuff."

But you ask the Union, and they will say,

"That stuff pays your wages." Interestingly enough, that's what the managers say too.

See? I'm not sure my strike was for the same reasons as my Union.

I went on strike for more time and less stuff and for a return to public service.

That seems to me to be the recipe for a happy life.

What follows is my letter to you, Granny Smith. My letter of apology for everything that has gone wrong with the Royal Mail.

2

Dawn Colours and Bird Song

I first started working for the Royal Mail in November 1979. I transferred from BT, which in those days, if you remember, was part of the same company. It was called the Post Office.

This was the same year Margaret Thatcher came to power, but before she started "selling off the family silver to pay for the servants", as Harold Macmillan so memorably put it.

It was a different job in those days. For a start we had proper training. I was trained for a whole week, going out and shadowing one postie, who taught me all the tricks of the trade: all the short cuts and the best way round every walk, how to pack my bag, how to bundle up the letters, how to do loops, where to leave my bike, what to look out for and what to avoid and where all the fierce dogs were. These days people are just thrown out onto the street without any training at all and if a dog goes for them, it's their own fault.

There was a four-man rota, covering three deliveries, with one man in reserve. It was a six-day week, seven hours and 40 minutes a day. Saturdays was "Job and Knock", meaning when you finished delivering on a Saturday you went home. It was a lighter day too, with no second delivery, so you were finished by 9.30. That's why we didn't mind the six-day week. It was almost as good as having the whole weekend off. Better, in fact, because we got an early start.

Start time then was 4.45. There was always someone already in when we arrived. This was the PHG: "Postman Higher Grade".

We don't have PHGs anymore. They abolished the grade a few years back. The PHG earned a few quid more than the rest of us, but then they decided to phase him out. His wages stopped increasing, and as the differential faded and the ordinary postie's pay started to catch up, as all the old PHGs retired, so the grade quietly slipped out of existence, like an old postman's cap dropped into a river and carried out to sea, and then slowly sinking beneath the waves.

Our last PHG was Bill. That was over

two years ago now.

But the PHG was important to the structure of the Royal Mail as it was. He wasn't management. He came up from the ranks. So he was like a sergeant major. He had more authority than the rest of us: a few more duties.

For instance, Bill was in charge of "the cage". This is the secure part of the office where the keys and the valuables are kept. It's called the cage because it is reinforced so no one can break into it. It is here, too, where we keep the Special Deliveries, that higher-priced premium mail in which you place valuable goods and documents and which is guaranteed to arrive by 1.00pm the next day. Us postmen have to sign to say we've received it, and then sign again if we have to return it.

At one time the PHG was in sole possession of the cage and no one had access to it without Bill's permission. These days there are at least half a dozen ordinary postmen who do the same job.

The PHG no longer exists, and there's no discipline any more. Bill was kind, stern and funny all at the same time.

He'd say, "Oi, oi, Mr Mayall" and call me over to the office for a ticking-off whenever I made a mistake, which I often did in the early days. And when he'd finished with me he'd say, "We'll learn you. We'll make a postman of you yet."

I loved old Bill, and I was even an assistant PHG for a while. That was before they abolished the grade, of course. These days there's nothing left to aspire to.

Anyway, as I say, we started work at 4.45.

First of all it was the internal sorting.

The mail came in in bags, and we'd

tip it all out and then sort it into all the original walks. There were more walks then, and more of us to do them. There was no junk mail in those days either, or very little. No advertising leaflets. No special offers. No mass mail-out catalogues. No charities begging for your cash. No generalised mail addressed to "The Householder" or "The Occupier". No surveys. No letters with pens in them to help you reply. No promises of a guaranteed free gift that always turns out to have strings attached. No garish envelopes offering cash prizes. No free draws. No miniaturised sachets containing free samples of hair conditioner. No free energy-saving light bulbs. No pizza adverts. No two-for-the-price-of-one deals.

No. In those days, there were letters, there were bills, there were bank statements; there were postcards and birthdays cards and anniversary cards; there were a few packages, some Special Deliveries and Recorded Deliveries; not much more. If we had one bag of mailsort a week we complained.

Let me explain what "mailsort" is. Actually, you would recognise it. It's a form of third class corporate mail, very cheap. It has a big "M" in the right-hand corner instead of the Queen's head, and is the means by which all this advertising comes through the post. If you want to know what to throw away, there's a fair chance it will have an "M" in the corner. Probably more than two-thirds of what we deliver these days is mailsort. Thirty years ago it hardly existed.

So sorting was finished fairly quickly: say in about an hour. Then we prepared our own rounds, slotting the letters into the individual addresses, before bundling up the mail, and putting it into a bag ready to go out.

That was at 6.45.

Notice I said "a bag". Not ten bags, which is what we take out these days. One bag. Admittedly it was a very full bag. There were no weight limits in those days either. We stuffed all the mail into one huge bag, piled up like the Leaning Tower of Pisa on the front of our bikes, and took it out. There were no drop-off points. No secure boxes where the mail was kept so you could pick up your extra bags. There were no extra bags.

I think this was probably different in the metropolitan areas. They did things differently in the city. But all of the rounds from our office were done on bikes, and we took them out in one load.

So, now, here's something I want you to imagine. Probably some of you are early risers, so you know what the world is like at that time of the morning. It depends on the time of year, of course, and the weather, but sometimes you'd go out of the office just as the sun was coming up, and it was like you were cycling through your own personal corner of Eden. That lovely soft, golden light of the early morning, listening to the birds singing, the suburban gardens all bursting with flowers. And there's just you, the milkman, a few dog-walkers and the occasional late-night reveller who's winding his way home from the night before.

As a postie you've already been up for two hours by now. You're fresh, in the peak of health. There's no traffic, no traffic fumes, just the wind bustling in from the coast, and the great, vast garden of the earth all around you.

It's like the whole earth has grown

bigger, like it has taken in a breath and expanded itself, is stretching itself to shake off the night.

See. That was what it was like. That was why posties were always so happy, why, if you said "good morning" to a postie, you would always get a cheery reply. I mean, I can't speak for everyone. Everyone is different, of course, but I seem to remember – and I don't think I'm imagining it – that us posties were amongst the happiest workers in the whole world.

So that's it. That's what I want you to imagine.

I want you to hear the song in a postie's heart as he slides your letters through the letter box. It's a song made up of dawn colours and bird song, and your letters are bathed in morning light.

That's what your postage stamp used to pay for. Not just getting a letter from

here to there, not just a delivery, but a little
spark of Eden.

3
Rainy Days

That was the round. It wasn't always as perfect as that, of course. Sometimes it was raining. Sometimes it was still dark. Sometimes the hail came crashing in from the North Sea like shot blasts from the ice caves of hell. The winds blow, the frosts descend, there's ice on the pavement. But we're a hardy lot, us posties. We take the sun and we take the rain. We take the hail, we take the snow. We take the winter and the summer. We watch the progress of the year through all of its seasons. We know what time of year it is by the stirring in our blood. We are always alive to the weather.

I've been out in every kind of weather. This is what makes me different to you. You early risers and dog-walkers, you late-night revellers coming home from your parties. Some days none of you are about. And then it's just me, wrapped up in my waterproofs, labouring against the wind, the rain lashing my face.

But, I tell you what: do you ever remember your mail being wet? In the old days, that is?

No, it never got wet. We had a waterproof tarpaulin bag which went over the mail bag and which tied up at the top, and your mail was snug and dry in there, and if it got wet at all, it was only from the wetness of our hands.

These days the bags let in water and we don't have time to shelter, so if it rains you get wet mail.

Just one more thing to apologise for.

Anyway, whatever the weather, the last letter was always delivered by 9.30.

You tell the kids that and they won't believe you. The post used to come before breakfast. You could read your mail with your morning tea. And it was real mail too. There were letters. You'd hear the snap of the letter box, and the sound of mail flopping onto the mat, and there would be a touch of excitement, of anticipation, at what might be in the post today.

I used to get letters maybe three or four times a month. Long letters from friends or family, from all over the country, and from abroad. Letters written by hand. It wasn't some generic font – Times New Roman, or Verdana — it was the real handwriting of the real person who was writing to me. You see, handwriting tells you something about a person. It tells you something about their mood. Something of their personality is in there, something of the person themselves. Those loops and curves and lines, those squiggles and dashes. And extravagant people would write extravagantly, and shy people would write shyly, and bold people would write boldly, and sometimes people who pretended to be bold but were in fact shy would show it in their handwriting.

Me: my handwriting was always crabby and tiny, filling up all of the space, because I never thought there was enough room on the page to say all I had to say.

So, now, we've delivered the last letter and it's back to the office, to the recreation room, and to a hearty breakfast. An hour's proper break. And we'd get in at the same time as all our mates. And there was a dartboard in the recreation room, and dominoes, and cards. We had all these leagues going. There'd be jokes and banter and what we saw on the telly last night, and "How's Spurs doing?" and "Your team aren't doing so well". You'd read the paper and drink a proper cup of tea, made in a teapot. So we had a real social life. And some of the guys were mates and some weren't. There'd be squabbles: that's just called being human. But generally we'd get on. It was a great atmosphere in the office.

And after an hour it was back to work, to the facing table.

This is where it gets really surprising.

You see, in those days there was an early morning collection. A van would go round and empty all the post boxes from the town, and instead of being taken over to the regional office, as it is now, it was all emptied out onto the facing table and sorted and franked there and then. So we'd sort out and bundle up the stuff for the Big City, which would go up on the train later that afternoon, all packed into mail bags. And we'd sort out the stuff for the main delivery office in the region, for all the nearby towns and villages, and that would go over by van. But any stuff for this town would stay in this office. And any first-class mail posted in the town that morning to be delivered in the town would go into the second post. So you could post a letter in the morning and have it delivered by the second post that same day. It was almost as fast as email.

4
Time

You ask me what has changed most
about the job in the 30 years I've been
here and I'll tell you. It is time.

We used to have time. Not just time for
ourselves: time for other people too.

We call you "Granny Smith" and that
nickname stems from the old days, because
we were always there for Granny Smith. We
had an idea of service. And if an old lady
was worried about something, we'd listen.

Sometimes we'd pick up the paper on the way to our round and we'd drop it off for her, or we'd run little errands for her if she was in need. We'd listen to her woes and her troubles and her joys and about what her grandchildren were up to and she'd offer us tea, and sometimes we'd accept it. We were a lifeline for Granny Smith: someone she knew would be arriving that day. And you could set your watch by the postie then. Always on the same road at the same time. Always the same postie, the same familiar face, a part of the family almost. And sometimes she'd know us by name, or if not, by our nickname, which is the name everyone calls us, and which we have always borne with pride.

"Postie".

So that's what you can call me now. "Postie". Everyone else does.

You see, this is what the new management at the Royal Mail don't get. They think we're a business in the market place, here to make money. And I have no objection to money or to making it. But being a postie is so much more than this, so much more than Gordon Brown or Peter Mandelson or Adam Crozier, or any of the other penny-pinching pen-pushers in offices and behind desks, with their figures and their targets and their profit and loss accounts, can ever imagine. What they don't know is that we are a part of the very fabric of our national life, we are the thread that binds the nation together, weaving our way from door to door, not just bringing the news, but bringing stability and service, confidentiality, comfort, a familiar face, and time to listen when required.

Time, Peter Mandelson. Time. That's what you are stealing. "Time is Money" you say, but I say "Time is Service". Time is listening. Time is being there, on time, so my customers know. Time is spending time on the things that matter, on the brief exchange of words that is the breath of life itself, sharing the air, shooting the breeze, enjoying the moment, taking a little time, before I pass on up the road and on my way.

How can you measure this?

Granny Smith is everyone. Everyone is vulnerable in the end. Everyone is someone's mother or father or sister or brother or uncle or cousin. Everyone needs someone. But if you are alone and vulnerable, if your family has gone, or moved away, who do you have left?

Just the postie. The postie bringing the mail.

I've seen it all in my time. There are some warden-assisted old persons' flats on my round. One day I came across an old lady who had fallen down. She'd knocked her zimmer frame over and couldn't get up to ring the alarm. She'd been there for about twenty minutes when I found her. So I helped her back up and into her flat and made her a cup of tea while she called the warden.

Another time I came to someone's door and I noticed it was ajar and the mail from the weekend was still on the mat. That worried me. I looked through the window and saw him there on the floor. I went in. I didn't have to force entry as the door was open. He was still breathing. I called an ambulance, covered him up with a coat, and then went and finished off delivering to the estate before the ambulance arrived. He died later that day.

Once I was there just after one of my customers had lost his wife. The neighbours came out and told me. He'd woken up that morning and when he turned to her she was dead. She'd died in her sleep. He used to come out every morning to collect his mail from a home-made mail box by the gate, always with a cheery greeting. He didn't come out for days after that, and then, when he did, he had tears in his eyes and I could do no more than say "I'm sorry".

But then later I could do more, you see. He kept getting letters addressed to his wife and he kept sending them back. I knew that this was distressing for him. So I spoke to him.

"Do you want me to get rid of these letters for you?" I asked.

"If you could. Yes please. I would be very grateful."

So whenever I saw a letter addressed to his wife I would put it back in my bag. And then later, in the office, I would return it. And these days he's back to collecting his mail from his mail box with a wave and a few cheery words about the weather again.

You see, I know my customers and they know me and in the old days I had a little time for them too. I still do. I make time, though there's no time for just shooting the breeze any more. But if someone is in need, I will still do whatever I can to help.

It's only human.

5

In the Office

I always say it's a job of two halves. The first half is in the office. It's loud and intense in here. There's real pressure to get everything done so you can get out. Everyone is shouting. There's a lot of noise. The radio is playing: usually some dumb local radio station reeling out mind-numbing hits from the sixties.

There's a lot of banter, a lot of swearing. Some of it is very quick, and very funny.

It's hard to give you a flavour of this as it's all "in the moment". People are working fast and talking fast at the same time.

But here's one sample, from the morning before the strike.

Alan: "Are you going to be on the picket line in the morning?"

Bob: "No, I'm going to be tucked up in bed with my lovely wife."

Colin: "I am though."

Bob: "What? You're going to be tucked up in bed with my lovely wife?"

Bob is the loudest and quickest of them all. There's a constant stream of banter emanating from his frame. His reactions are instantaneous and often hilarious. He's like a one-man comedy routine, with a string of catchphrases which he repeats endlessly and always with exactly the same relish. He also has a tendency to burst into a raucous chorus of "If I Were A Rich

Man". That or any of a dozen other songs. He has the look of a naughty boy just about to play some prank on you. Often there's a perverse element to it. One of his tricks is to drop his trousers to his knees when he's in the urinal, like a little boy having a pee by the roadside. He does this to every un-suspecting new employee and it will usual-ly cause screams of protest. This, of course, is exactly what he's looking for.

Let's set the scene. Tread carefully. We are now about to enter the men's toilets.

Jim is there, just about to have a pee. It's the same day: the morning before the strike. I'm there. We're lined up like prop-er men in a toilet, looking blankly at the wall in front. There are one or two others, washing their hands, or just on their way out. It is the busy time, just before we're about to set out on our rounds. Bob en-ters. Only he's not just undoing his zip:

he's unbuckling his belt too, starting to pull down his trousers. There's a look in his eye, perverse and playful at the same time. Jim screams in panic. "No, no, I don't want to see it!" he shouts, quickly pulling up his zip and rushing for one of the water closets to hide. Bob is too quick and has already dropped his trousers and is now backing into the closet with him, mooning at him. "Is it clean?" he says, amid raucous laughter. "I want you to tell me if it's clean or not."

It's not all as good-humoured as this, however. Sometimes the pressure gets very intense and tempers get frayed. This is particularly true when management make one of their arbitrary decisions, favouring one of the compliant posties over the rest of us. This is a common occurrence. There is deliberate provocation: one of the "favoured" postmen being allowed to leave before all the rest of us, who are being held back in the office waiting for the mis-sort run. This is the van that goes over to the city to collect any late mail. Often we're standing around waiting for it to arrive. Sometimes, when it gets back, there are only one or two additional items of mail, sometimes none at all. Management know we're eager to get out but hold us back anyway. There's a duty to deliver all mail, they say. But then, if it suits them, they will hold back the mail. Or they will let someone on overtime go out and not wait for the mis-sorts. There's an element of favouritism and a feeling that the rules are being applied arbitrarily, to suit management, and not fairly, to suit everyone.

There's a lot a resentment and an increasing amount of bullying. There's a feeling that they are trying to wind everyone up, to get rid of as many full-timers as possible. It has become so persistent, so noticeable, we believe it is a deliberate policy, being driven from higher up. The old posties have to go, to be replaced by part-timers and casuals.

One of the current tricks is in the application of the so-called "Attendance Procedure".

Believe it or not, sometimes posties are made to come into work even if they are sick or injured, on threat of dismissal.

The Attendance Procedure is the means by which this is done.

They monitor your attendance. You are only allowed a certain amount of absences in any one year. If you exceed the number of absences you are brought before management and a so-called Stage One warning is issued. This is regardless of whether your illness is genuine or not. Every absence is considered to be genuine, but each one is also counted towards the Attendance Procedure, regardless of how long you were away. A day or a week, it makes no difference. The limits are: no more than two illnesses in a year, and no more than three weeks' absence. If you exceed the limits a second time, a Stage Two warning is issued. A third time, it's Stage Three and possible dismissal. There is no right of appeal against either Stage One or Stage Two and although they are meant to be discretionary, discretion is never used. This, of course, is the exact opposite of the meaning of the word "discretion".

So by Stage Two, a person is already under threat of dismissal. One more warning and that's it: you're on your way out.

So no matter how ill you are, if you are on a Stage Two you daren't miss work. I've seen people hauled up before management because they were in hospital for a hernia operation and have exceeded the total number of days allowed off in any one year. And I've heard of people on the verge of a mental breakdown being bullied and harassed and humiliated in front of the entire office and sent home crying like babies. This is happening more and more at the Royal Mail.

Everything is arse-about-face. Words have come to mean their exact opposite. So "discretion" means "mandatory". And "flexibility" means "as directed". I have to be flexible at work, meaning I have to do what I'm told. Management can twist the rules at will. They can apply the rules in one case and ignore them in another. And meanwhile we have young managers of no more than a few months' experience overriding old posties who have been in the job for 30 years.

Take this as an example.

A few weeks ago, a new, young manager came into the office and, as a way of flexing his muscles, told us that we could no longer leave our mail bags under our frames. It was "a health and safety issue" he said.

Pardon?

I've been leaving my bags under my frame since I got here and I haven't tripped over them once. How can I trip over them? They're under the frame, for God's sake.

But — so be it — we do as we are told. So you can picture us now: a whole office full of confused postal workers waving their mail bags around in the air wondering what to do with them. Where are we supposed to put them? On top of the frame? That's where the packets go. On the work surface? That's where the letters go. Beside the frame? That would cause precisely the health and safety issue that is the excuse for this little exercise in futility. There's nowhere else to put them. So, eventually, after a week of stumbling over our exposed bags in the name of "health and safety", they go back to where they've always been: under the frame, out of the way.

The way it's always been.

6

The Memory Waltz

This job is more difficult than you would imagine.

Maybe you think, "What's so hard about posting a few letters? You read the envelope, you look at the door; if the door matches the envelope, you push it through."

True.

That's the easy part.

The difficult part is in the preparation. It's in learning your "frame".

The frame is the postie's workstation. It varies in size depending on the size of the round, on the number of addresses you have to deliver to. Town centre rounds with lots of terraced streets, with doors close by each other, are larger than rural or suburban rounds, with lots of gates and lots of drives and lots of walking between them. Rural rounds are usually driven. Town centre rounds are usually walked. Suburban rounds are usually done on a bike.

The frame is divided up firstly by road, and then by number. Each address has a different slot. This would be easy if it was laid out logically, say 2, 4, 6, 8 on one side, and 1, 3, 5, 7 on the other. But that's not how it works. The frame is laid out as you would walk it. So you might do a loop, up one side and down the other. Up to number 23, and down again to 2. And then up again up to number 37, and down again to number 24. Or you might walk along one road, and take a turning into another, and then back to the first road again, and then into another. Some long roads are divided up all over the frame. So it's not just a matter of remembering where the road is, it's a matter of remembering where certain numbers on that road are, and where the roads are divided.

Being a postie is above all else a feat of memory.

My round has thirteen roads, which I divide up in a variety of different ways.

The roads are scattered about all over the frame.

So my day starts with "throwing off" my frame. I pick a letter from a bundle, I read the address, and I slot it into the frame. And then I do it again. And again. And again. I have 600 addresses on my frame. Some addresses may have ten or fifteen letters, some may have none. I can't tell you how many letters I throw off every day. But I can give you some weights. I usually take out about six bags, generally between fourteen and sixteen kilos each. You can work it out. That's a lot of letters.

You do this for about fifteen minutes, from 6.15 to 6.30, and then again for about an hour, from 7.45 till you're ready to go out.

You get into a sort of rhythm while throwing off your frame. You read the letter, you slot it in. You read the next letter, you slot it in. And on, and on. My frame is about six foot high by six foot across, with two "wings" reaching out to surround me, like the arms of an embrace.

There's a work surface piled up with letters and bundles at about waist height. You pick up a bundle, read off the addresses and slot them into your frame. You have to shuffle back and forth across the length of your frame to do this. Some of the addresses are about waist height, while others are above your head. To the left. To the right. On the wings. So you're moving about, back and forth, turning at the waist, throwing your arms in the air, trying to remember where all the addresses are. You are soft-shoe shuffling across the floor, listening to the radio, reading the addresses, sliding the letters into the appropriate slot. I call this The Mnemonic Shuffle, the Memory Waltz. You are dancing with your own memory.

Sometimes you forget where an address is. Then you tap the letter on the frame to remind yourself. You tap the letter on the side of your head. You tap your foot. You click your tongue. You tut and you mumble. And then you remember, and a whole new flow of numbers starts up.

You keep on doing this until all the letters are in the frame. After this you do the "flats". Flats are large letters and magazines, A4 size and above. And after this you do the packets. Smaller packets you sort into the frame. Larger packets you put on top of your frame and you turn a letter in the frame to mark it. When you come to a turned letter on your round you know there's a packet to be delivered.

After this you do the redirections, weeding out those letters for people who have recently moved. After this you bundle up the letters into the order you are going to take them out in and put them into bags. This can take up to an hour, depending on the weight of mail that day. You take the bags over to the scales and weigh them. Then you put the bags that are to go out with the drivers into a large, rattling metal container called a "york". The yorks are like cages on wheels. The drivers collect the bags from the yorks and take them out to the collection points. The rest of the bags you load onto your bike. I usually have a large bag on the front, a small bag over my shoulder, and several bundles and packets in my panniers on the back.

After this you go out.

The other part of the job is Internal Sorting. This takes place before you throw off your frame, soon after you come into the office, from about 6.30 till 7.45. This is where you sort all the letters into their individual rounds. This is done collectively. All the full-time posties have to do this.

This, again, is a feat of memory. It is even more complex and baroque than learning your frame. Now you have to know every road in the office, and which frame each road belongs to. You have to read the address and know that, say, number 7

Arbitrary Walk is on frame 13, and that number 2 Existential Parade is on frame 23. Some roads go across several frames. There are pigeon holes for each round in the office, each with a corresponding frame. There are notices above the pigeon holes with a list of all the roads that are delivered from your office, in alphabetical order, with a number to say which frame it's on.

There are – I don't know – maybe 150 roads being sorted from this office, into, say, 40 frames.

You try reading from an alphabetical list of 150 road names and working out where the letter is supposed to go. From Agamemnon Street to Xerxes Avenue, including the saints' names which all begin the same: St James Road, St Jerome Walk, St Judas Square, St Barnabas Boulevard.

Then you try memorising it.

But you do in the end. Every road on every frame is ground into your consciousness by years of sorting, till, in the end, you can almost do it with your eyes closed. After that you can sort and talk at the same time.

I have an image to explain how this happens.

When I first started doing this job I used to deliver to an estate. It was a brand-new estate at the time. I would park my bike at the entrance and do the whole thing in two bundles, round one way, and then round the other, going back to my bike to collect the second bundle.

About halfway through the second part of the estate there was a sudden turning, down some steps, to the right, to the left, and into a sort of covered walkway with two doors. And dangling from the roof of the walkway between the doors was a hanging basket. I would post my letters into the first door, turn, walk, then bang my head against the hanging basket. Almost every day I did that, for about two weeks. And every day I cursed myself and that stupid hanging basket. And then, after that, I learned to duck.

That's all this job is really.

It's like banging your head over and over again.

And then learning how to duck.

7
Out on the Round

Now I want to take you out on my round.

This is the best part of the job, and is the reason why us postal workers continue to do what we do.

We all love this part.

Indeed, I often think, in my paranoid moments, that it is precisely because we like our job so much that the gods of power and economics – whoever they are who are running the show — have decided to mess it up for us.

"Look: there's a happy bunch of workers. We'll have to put a stop to that!"

It's hard to say what the pleasure is. It's very hard work. We carry a lot of weight. Our bikes are very heavy. They are built of granite and red kryptonite and would probably survive a direct nuclear hit. And then we fill them up with mail. There's mail in the tray on the front, two bags' worth, piled high: probably as much as we used to carry for our entire round 30 years ago. There's mail in the panniers at the back. Mail in a bag on our shoulders. Mail on the rack at the back. And we haul this huge weight from the office to the beginning of the round, straining our knees and our hips to do so.

But after this, of course, the weight is going down. Bit by bit, letter by letter, door by door, the weight is diminishing. And we're out in the fresh air, on our own, no one looking over our shoulders, with enough time, even now, to get to know the people on our rounds. So it's sociable and solitary at the same time. And despite the fact that we are walking over the same bit of ground every day, through the same streets, past the same houses, it is our own unique and special corner of God's great creation. It is our territory. It matters to us.

And the weather is different every day. And although the people are the same, the conversations are different. And even now, late as it is, overworked and weary as we can become, there's a real sense of joy, of engagement with the world, of accomplishment, of getting on with the day's business, which is the important task of getting the mail through.

I start my round on Valley Road: up one side and down the other, in two bundles, with any parcels in the bag on my shoulder.

Mr Jones lives at the top end of the road. I don't know how old he is: in his eighties at least. He's usually standing at the kitchen window when I come up the road. He's looking out for me. When I get to the point where I have to cross the road to get to Mr Jones's house, I will indicate whether I have mail for him or not. A shake of the head means no, otherwise I'll hold the letter up to show him what he's got. By the time I've crossed the road, he's made it to the front door and is waiting for me.

"Aren't you supposed to be on strike?" he says. You won't believe the number of times I've heard that. It's because the Union have called a series of one-day strikes over several days, and everyone is confused.

"Tomorrow," I say, and hand him his Sky Magazine.

"What's this?" he says, looking disdainfully at the cover. "I never read it."

"Why do you get it then?"

"I don't know. I suppose I'm privileged because I get Sky."

"You like Sky then?"

"Oh yes. It stops me going down the drain," he says, laughing in a self-mocking way.

We have a conversation like this almost every day, a few seconds' banter before I get on with my round.

It was Mr Jones who initiated this daily routine. One day, when I first started doing this round, he came to the door to greet me.

"I always like to see the postman," he said. "It makes me feel that everything's right with the world."

It's moments like this when I know how important my job is. It's not just delivering the mail: it's being a valued and trusted member of the community. It's helping people to keep in touch. It's keeping an eye on people's houses and making sure everything's OK. It's knowing people and who they are. It's being, in some cases, their friend.

Next up the road is Mr Dawson. If he's expecting a letter he'll already be at the door. The pretext is that he's polishing his brass letter box. The door will be open, and he'll be bending down, a cloth in his hand. I was faintly amused at his impatient waiting at first, until I realised how important it was to him. He is waiting for a hospital appointment.

Unfortunately all I have to hand over today is a letter from a charity and a handful of door-to-door leaflets.

I carry bags full of this kind of rubbish every day. Some people don't even have the decency to address the mail they're sending out. This is the stuff we call "door-to-door" or "household". You call it junk mail.

It arrives by the boxload: all these over-sized bits of glossy paper or card advertising this or that useless gizmo that nobody wants and nobody needs. No one pays any attention to it. No one bothers to read it. It goes straight through the door and into the bin.

This is the most embarrassing thing about my job. There's Mr Dawson, waiting on a letter that could mean life or death, and all I have to hand over is a begging letter and a bunch of slick, silly adverts.

Mr Dawson looks at the letter from the charity. "What's this?" he says. "Last week they were begging for orphans. This week it's for animals."

"I'm sorry," I say, and then move on.

I'm doing this for about four hours: full pelt, non-stop.

The first bag takes about an hour and a half to two hours, depending on the weight of the mail that day; the next two bags take about an hour each. I'm always massively overweight. I do thirteen roads, including blocks of flats and an old people's home. There are nearly 600 delivery points on my round: that's letter boxes to you. Sometimes there are gates and gardens to negotiate, sometimes it's terraced streets. I look into your front window as I approach.

There's a cliché about us postmen: the picture of us being chased up the garden path by a ferocious dog taking a bite out of our pants. Unfortunately, that's very nearly the truth. Dogs hate us, with good reason. It reveals something about our relationship to you.

We are intrusive in your lives. We push something through your letter box. We get quite close to you without you knowing, and we learn a lot about you on the way. We know who's left who for another man. Who is divorced, who is single. We know if your son is estranged from you. We know when it's your birthday or your wedding anniversary or when there's been a death in the family. We know where your Aunt Vera went on her holiday and we know that she wished you were there.

We also know when you are away.

We are in a position of great responsibility in relation to you and your property.

That's the trouble with all the arguments for the casualisation of mail delivery: they don't take this into account.

It is being fuelled by the demand of the corporations for faster and cheaper mail, not by the demand of the consumer, for security in their homes.

Sometimes we get thieves amongst us, it's true: people who steal from the mail. People who steal your credit cards, or open your birthday cards to see if there's any cash in them. They always get caught in the end. When one man does one round, the customers notice, and they know who it is.

Once the mail is broken up, once the postie has been stripped of his round, once the relationship between a postal worker and his customer has been destroyed, then what?

Then it will be the end of the security of your mail.

8

Team Talk

Every Tuesday we have something called a "Team Talk".

This is a euphemism, as there is no team, and no one talks.

Us posties just sit there and listen. We chew our nails. We fiddle with our pens. We scratch our arses. We take sips from our coffee, bought just before the proceedings from the vending machine outside. We glance idly round the room to see what's changed.

Once upon a time this was the recreation room. We used to play cards and darts in here. There was a kitchen. You could make a cup of tea or coffee, fry up some bacon, have a bacon sandwich. Also, back in the old days there was a tea club. Before the job was contracted out, when the cleaners all used to be ex-posties, they would collect money every week, and then they'd come round to your frames and ask you what you would like. "Tea? Coffee? How would you like it? One sugar or two?" No vending machines then. Teas and coffees brought to your frame.

That was what this room was used for back then. For making teas and coffees in. For recreation. For sociability. For friendship. For banter. For reading newspapers. For relaxing. For chatting. For asking after each other's health. For ordinary, unremarkable things that seem like a privilege now.

Nowadays it's only used for Team Talk.

The reason we have Team Talk on a Tuesday is that Tuesday is a light day. Mail delivery is a variable business. No two days are the same. Wednesdays and Thursdays are generally heavy days. Mondays and Fridays are average days. Saturday used to be a light day, but has now become a heavy day. We used to leave all the mailsort behind on a Saturday, but these days a lot of the mailsort has been replaced by downstream access mail from the private companies: people like TNT and CityLink. So Saturdays aren't so light any more.

But Tuesdays are. Tuesdays are still light.

This is because all the sorting machines in the big metropolitan offices are turned off on Sunday. Nothing passes through the mail system on a Sunday. And come Tuesday this has filtered down to all the delivery offices.

So instead of sorting mail and delivering it, on Tuesday we have Team Talk.

It's like going back to your childhood: to school assembly.

The manager stands in front of you and makes various announcements. Sometimes he even tries to make you join in.

"So, now everyone, hands up, what exactly do we mean by 'modernisation'?"

We just shuffle about, yawn, tap our feet. What we'd really like to do is get on with our rounds, get the mail out, and go home a little early for a change. Instead of which we are subjected to propaganda.

Because that's what it is really. Team Talk is our weekly propaganda session. Workers' education. Workers' re-orientation. A chance to fill our heads with corporate drivel.

Don't ask me what they are talking about half the time. I'm not paying attention. We get facts and figures and targets. One thing I do remember on a regular basis is a lecture on safety and how to ride your bike.

We're not supposed to bump up and down curbs. We're not supposed to carry mail in our hands. We're not supposed to ride one-handed. We're not supposed to scoot our bikes on the pavement. We're not supposed to carry too much weight. We're not supposed to balance mail on our racks. We're not supposed to carry a mail bag over our shoulder. We're supposed to wear a cycle helmet at all times when the bike is in motion.

You'll have to try to imagine this last point. The helmets are uncomfortable: too hot in summer, cold and wet in winter, so we tend to take them off once we are on our rounds. This is annoying enough as it is, as the helmet gets in the way of the mail, filling up the panniers, or bouncing along on the back of the rack; and we all know that the rule about helmets isn't being instituted for our benefit, but to protect Royal Mail in case of an accident. It's Royal Mail abiding by statutory Health and Safety regulations. It's so Royal Mail can say they have done everything to promote Health and Safety.

But, now, imagine: we have to put the helmet on every time the bike is in motion.

We get off our bikes. We pick out a bundle then deliver it. We get back on our bikes. We cycle to the next stopping point. We get off our bikes again. We deliver another bundle. And on, and on. How many times a day would we be taking off our helmets and putting them back on again?

It's the same with the other rules: not scooting on pavements, not bumping up and down the curb, not cycling one-handed. If we followed these rules we would never be home before teatime.

So, of course, when we are sitting in Team Talk listening to this, we know, and they know — we all know — that none of it will be implemented. We know that if we did this we would be late every day and then hauled up before the manager for "wilful delay".

We know they are just filling the time.

9

Modernisation

More recently, however, they've been talking about serious things. They've been talking about "modernisation".

It's an interesting word, that.

Modernisation.

Just roll it around the tongue once or twice. We have to be modern, don't we? Who wouldn't want to be modern?

Actually, it's just another euphemism, like "flexibility" or "discretionary".

"Modernisation" means scaling back the service in order to serve the interests of the corporations. It means "profitability" which means "cutting costs" which means "cutting back on fixed expenditures" which means – and I don't have to employ inverted commas for this – lower standards and lower wages.

That's the future. That's what being "modern" is all about.

And in between all this we are spoon-fed examples of what this modernisation programme will involve.

Mostly it involves the introduction of new technology. Once again, who can argue with this? New technology is a good thing, right? It's, like, computers and stuff. It's faster and it will make our job easier.

So, now, let me give you some real samples of what the Royal Mail have lined up for us.

Welcome to the future, folks.

This is what it will look like:

ELECTRIC TROLLEYS. We are all going to be issued with electric trolleys. Bikes obviously aren't modern enough. So we are all going to walk around following an electric trolley which will go at a uniform speed. Will the trolley stop or are we supposed to keep up? Apparently they've already been trialled in some parts of the country. Problem is, they're too big for the pavements, so they have to go on the road. Problem with this is they violate all parking laws. The Royal Mail might find themselves being issued with tickets for "illegally parked electric trolleys".

Also, in the places where the trolleys have been trialled, the round has been extended, from three and a half hours to four. Three and a half hours already means four and a half hours, so four hours will mean five. You can see the thinking behind this. The electric trolley takes the weight so the postie can work for longer. One man can do more work, a cost-saving benefit to the corporations when they take over the running of the Royal Mail.

Of course, this brings up all sorts of issues. Like: if the electric trolleys go at walking speed, how do we get them to the round? Some rounds are many miles from the office. A bike can go fast, and it can go slow. A bike can get you to the round quickly, and then still serve as a trolley once you're there.

So the trolleys will have to be taken over by van. Currently Royal Mail vans are too small to take the trolleys, so, obviously, a new fleet of vans is required. Also, what about maintenance? All the bikes in our office are currently maintained by one man. They are simple and efficient machines, with replaceable parts. The wheel goes, he puts on a new wheel. The stand goes, he puts on a new stand. Will the electric trolleys ever be this straightforward? Will they have to retrain the bike maintenance men so that they can fix the electric trolleys, or will the electric trolly maintenance have to be contracted out? And how much will all of this cost? Will the taxpayer pay for all of this, only to have the Royal Mail handed over to a corporation in the end?

"STARBURST". The person who invented this name obviously has theatrical tendencies. It sounds like the name of a musical, or of an interstellar vehicle in some big-budget Hollywood science fiction movie.

The idea is that we will all go out on delivery in the backs of vans in teams. We will burst from the back of the van with our pre-packed bags (all singing and dancing, no doubt, to the "Starburst" theme) and then scatter, delivering as we go. The vans will carry lots of spare bags of mail, and the posties will follow the vans up and down the roads. A bit like the way bin men currently work, a team of guys following a big van. Only this will be in reverse. We bring you your rubbish, the bin men take it away again.

Obviously, the advantage of this is that you can use casual workers to do it. There's no skill involved, no feats of memory. Old-time posties who know the frames can be kept in the office to serve the new teams of casual postal workers who just have to be chucked out on the street and told to deliver. And you can imagine them, can't you, starting the day with a collective "huddle" in which they close heads like an American football team while exhorting each other to greater efforts?

Perhaps they could all be made to wear name badges. "Hi, I'm Tim. Have a nice day."

And we could change the name of the Royal Mail too. We could call it "McMail". It has a certain ring.

Again, there's an obvious flaw in this. It removes the traditional relationship between a postie and his round. My uniform allows me to approach your house without suspicion. Specifically, I know when you are away. The question then is: who do you want wandering up your garden path and peering into your front windows: an old familiar face who has been serving you and your family for years, or a bunch of Mc-Posties who come bursting out of a van every morning?

DOUBLE-DECKER LORRIES AND LATER DELIVERY TIMES. Double-decker lorries are already in use in some parts of the country. You can see the reasons why they were brought in. Only one lorry in the place of two. Obvious savings.

Unfortunately, they also take twice as long to fill up, and as the mail isn't always ready at exactly the same time, often the lorries are leaving half-empty. Whoops. Double-decker lorries carrying the same amount of mail as single-decker lorries: someone hasn't been thinking everything through properly.

So now the idea is that the lorries will have to leave later to allow them to get filled up properly, which will put back start times for the rest of the postal service too. That's right, folks: modernisation in this case means later start times, yet again. A new suggested start time for delivery workers of 7.00am will mean that no one will leave the office till 10.30 at the earliest, which will mean last delivery at 3.00pm or even later.

WALKING SPEEDS. A few months back, if you remember, there was talk about posties having to increase the speed at which they walk: from 2.7mph on average, to 4mph.

This would save the Royal Mail millions, we were told.

I know exactly where this came from.

There's a computer programme called Pegasus which is supposed to measure how long each walk will take. You put in all the facts and figures and then a little computer-generated man walks through a little computer-generated walk – at 2.7mph no doubt – and, when it's run its course, it tells you how long it should take to do your round.

It estimated my round at three hours. It actually takes between four and five hours to complete, occasionally more.

That's where that walk-speed estimate came from: from someone in an office somewhere playing with Pegasus, working out that if they increased the speed of the little computer-generated man he could do even more computer-generated work.

Of course, real posties do not walk at 2.7mph. We scoot, we ride, we jog, we do loops, we get on our bikes and we get off again, we stop to deliver parcels and get signatures for Special Delivery and Recorded Delivery items, and, when the person isn't in, we write them a card telling them that they should pick it up at the office. We need to stop for a pee or a tea-break occasionally. Sometimes we even like to ask after the customer's health. And we do all of this at breakneck speed.

We couldn't go any faster.

"Pegasus": that's a mythological flying horse, isn't it?

I could do with one of those.

WALK SEQUENCING MACHINES. This, of course, is the *tour de force* of the whole modernisation programme. The Royal Mail currently already owns a complete national infrastructure of Walk Sorting Machines. These are machines that read the post-codes and sort out the mail according to the rounds. When I get in in the morning, there are already a number of pre-sorted bundles waiting for me. The bulk of the mail has by now been broken down into individual rounds, allowing me to begin throwing off my frame immediately.

A Walk Sequencing Machine takes this process one step further. Not only is the mail broken up into rounds, but the pre-sorted bundles are already sequenced so I can throw them all off in order. The machines can be programmed to the individual roads and the individual houses. All I have to do is look at the first address, then it's: 1, 3, 5, 7, 9, 11, 13 Relativity Crescent, followed by 2, 4, 6, 8, 10, 12 etc

You can see the advantage of this, and there's not a postie in the whole world who would object.

Trouble is, they don't work.

Or rather, to be absolutely precise about this, they work a bit, but not all that well. They speed things up, but not all that much.

Once again they are being trialled. They were due to be introduced in October 2008, but so far they still only exist in their original trial offices. There are all sorts of problems with them. Walk Sequencing Machines can't cope with differently shaped packets or obscure handwriting or other human factors, and much of the job still has to be done the old-fashioned way. In the end, the actual time-saving each of these multi-million pound machines provides is, on average, about seven minutes per round.

I have to apologise now for some unpleasant language. The operative terms here are "mech-ed" and "mech-able". Mech-ed mail is mail that has already been sorted through the machine. Mech-able mail is mail that is capable of being sorted. The aim was to get as much as 80 per cent of the mail mech-ed by now but the figure is much more like 50 per cent. There is a lot of mech-able mail, but not many mechanisms to mech it with.

Which, roughly translated, means that there's been an almighty cock-up, and while the Royal Mail has lost, removed, or frittered away large numbers of its staff (up to 30 per cent in the last two years) it has not replaced them with the requisite number of machines.

Or maybe – or am I being too paranoid here? – all of this is being done on purpose in order to run the Royal Mail down, in order to make it fail, so that when, eventually, it is sold off to a private company, it can be bought for a song. After which, of course, when the new methods are rolled out, and the new, slimmer, faster, corporate McMail takes over, and share prices begin to soar, it is those who hold the most shares who will make the most profit.

I wonder who that might be?

It won't be Tom, that's for sure.

10
Tom and Jerry

Tom was already working in the office when I started. He'd been here since 1970. He'd started off as a Telegram Boy at the age of fifteen. That was way back in the mid-fifties. Then he'd become a postman, and after that a driver, hauling the mail around the City in those big old Bedford vans. He did that for about twenty years before finally moving here.

Tom was a proper old postman. Totally

dedicated to his customers. He got to know them like friends.

He told me the story of the time he'd saved someone's life.

Her name was Mrs Brewer. Tom always used to knock on her door to see if she was all right. That was in the days when we had the time for such things. And then, one day, she didn't answer. He looked in through the letter box, but couldn't see her. He was a bit worried. So he looked through the window and he could see her through the net curtains. She was on the floor. He knew her sister, who lived just up the road. So Tom went to her sister's house, and then they both went back with the keys. Poor old Mrs Brewer had fallen down and couldn't get back up. When the ambulance came they said that Tom had saved her life.

Mind you, it didn't last long. It was the second time she'd fallen down like this.

They took her into hospital and later Tom went to see her. She told him they wanted to take her into a care home because she could no longer look after herself. She was very distressed. She said she liked where she lived and she didn't want to move.

Then she said a puzzling thing.

"Don't bother to come and see me again, Tom, 'cos I won't be here."

When he got home he told his wife.

"What did she mean by that?" he said.

"I know," said the wife.

She died that night. She died rather than move out of her home and into a care home.

Tom was full of stories like that.

But they were great times back then. We had a proper social life. Not just at work: we used to meet up after work too. Tom had a young family then. There were several posties' families with kids all about the same age and in the nearby town there was a social club. All of the families would meet up there a few times a year, especially at Christmas. There was one pub which was known as our pub. The posties' pub. We would all meet up there, the blokes and their wives. And on other occasions the wives and the kids would get together too. It was a proper community.

Tom's wife used to tell a funny story. Tom's round was adjacent to where he lived, which was also not far from another postie's round: Phil. And they used to meet up for their morning break at Tom's place. Only, because of the different directions of their rounds, Phil used to come in through the back door and Tom used to come in through the front; and then, later on, they would both leave by their respective doors, looking happy and relaxed after their break.

"I don't know what the neighbours thought," said Tom's wife, laughing.

Tom finally left the Royal Mail in 2005 after a lifetime of dedication to the service. His last fifteen years were spent on the same round. Everyone knew him by name, and when he left he had hundreds of cards and presents.

Jerry is a much younger man with a family, still working for the Royal Mail. He has three kids: two teenagers and a seven-year-old. One in college and two at school.

Jerry lives on tax credits because his wages aren't enough to cover his costs. He does no overtime because this would impact on his benefits. He hasn't had a holiday in years. He has no social life — he can't afford it — and the job is so exhausting he hardly has a family life either. By 7.30 he's falling asleep, and by 9.00 he's in bed.

That's all his life consists of: work and sleep.

Jerry is a good man, but worn down with the job. He used to be much more light-hearted and funny, full of jokes and quips and a non-stop dialogue with his own quirky, comic-book sense of humour. He was like a character out of the *Beano*. He looks much more brooding of late. If you talk to him now he just sounds weary. He fully expects to be working for a private company before he retires.

You have to ask why this should be. What has changed in the last 50 years? Why is Jerry's future so different from the one that Tom would have expected at the same age? How come Tom can rest in contented retirement, while Jerry only has a future full of hardship and uncertainty to look forward to?

Us posties haven't changed. Jerry is

as committed to his customers as Tom ever was. He is as dedicated, as honest, as straightforward, as hard-working, as decent, as kind. The post hasn't changed. We still need the post. So why are the workers suffering in this way?

I guess you might say, "It's the same for everyone. No one has any certainty any more."

I guess that's true.

But you still have to ask: why? What is the driving force behind all these changes?

Jerry says, "It's like the last days of the Roman Empire in here. Everyone's geared up for change. It's intense; new managers all the time, new little ways of doing things. It's falling to bits, everyone can see it. We can't even deliver a proper service to our customers any more. It's like a baker's shop with no cakes: a postal service that can't deliver the mail."

You can feel the Royal Mail crumbling all around you, he says, like a great edifice whose foundations are being systematically weakened. The foundations of the Royal Mail are its postal workers, the postmen and women who deliver the mail on a daily basis. It is the postal workers who are being undermined.

Jerry says, "We build up a rapport with our customers. They trust you. They don't like agency workers. Agency workers don't care and our customers don't know who they are. It's a case of caring. We are the face of Royal Mail, out on the streets every day, talking to the customers. We do care."

Jerry thinks it's sabotage. They want to wreck the Royal Mail, to run it into the ground so they can sell it off, he says. And they want to kill the Union.

"Divide and conquer," he says. "The managers are all on bonuses to come up with this stuff. They want us to modernise but they don't give us the tools to do it. We can't implement modernisation without the tools. Like: there aren't enough trolleys to go round. The hierarchy aren't concerned. They want it to fail."

Jerry is pessimistic about the future of the Royal Mail.

11
Grey Boxes

It was Jerry who started counting the contents of the grey boxes.

The grey boxes are the boxes that the mail comes in. They are about twelve inches wide and eighteen inches long and nine inches deep; stackable, so you can pile them up, one on top of another, without crushing the contents.

Ordinary letters are placed in vertically, facing the front, while A4 letters and magazines are carried flat. Hence the nick-name for this kind of mail. We call them "flats".

Almost everything has a nickname. We carry large volumes of mail around in containers called "yorks", and smaller volumes in "coffins". We call mailsort "rebate" and first-class mail "live mail". We call our rounds "walks" and we collect our bags at "drop-off points". We call our customers "Granny Smith".

Almost the only objects that don't have a nickname are the grey boxes. That's all they are: the grey boxes. The mail is delivered in them. We carry the mail around in them. When we're finished with them we stack them up.

The grey boxes are also the means by which we measure the volume of mail that is passing through the offices, and therefore through the Royal Mail as a whole.

In the past this was done by weight. Everything that came into the office was weighed. More recently it has been done by averages. There is an average for the number of letters the boxes are supposed to contain, agreed on by the Royal Mail and the Union in consultation. That figure was put at 208.

So that's how volumes were estimated: the number of boxes carried through each office, times 208.

You'll all know by now that both the Royal Mail and the government have been claiming that mail volumes are down.

The figure is usually put at ten per cent. That's a strangely exact figure. Peter Mandelson went on TV in May 2009 and said that it was due to competition from the electronic media, such as texts and email.

"Figures are down," he said.

You should have heard the hoots of

derision coming from mail centres and delivery offices up and down the country when he said that. Thousands of simultaneous splutters of astonishment and annoyance.

We hear the same phrase in the office almost every day. It's like a mantra.

"Figures are down."

You tell that to my back, which aches from the weight of it. You tell it to my hip, which creaks with every step. You tell it to my knees when they are labouring with the weight of the bike up a slope.

"Figures are down."

So how come it takes an extra half an hour to get out in the mornings these days? Why does it take longer to throw off my frame? And how does that account for the increased weight I am recording in the logbook every day? Me and every other postie?

We all look at each other in disbelief.

"You could have fooled me," we say.

Of course, this might be some kind of an accounting trick. They say figures are down, but does this take deregulation into account?

Deregulation is the result of an EU directive that was meant to be implemented over an extended period to give mail companies time to adjust, but which this government embraced with almost obscene relish, deregulating the UK mail service long before any of its rivals in Europe.

It means that any private mail company – or, indeed, any of the state-owned, subsidised European mail companies – is able to bid for Royal Mail contracts.

Take a look at your letters next time you pick them up from your mat. Look at the right-hand corner, the place where the

Queen's head used to be. You'll see a variety of different franks, representing a number of different mail companies. There's TNT, UKMail, CityMail, and a number of others. What these companies do is bid for the profitable bulk mail and city-to-city trade of the big companies, undercutting the Royal Mail in the process, and then have the Royal Mail deliver it for them. So TNT (the Dutch national mail company) have the very lucrative BT contract, for instance. TNT picks up all of BT's mail from the main offices, sorts it into individual walks according to information supplied by the Royal Mail, scoots it on to the mail centres in bulk, where it is then sorted and handed over to us to deliver.

Royal Mail does the work. TNT takes the profit.

By the way, TNT also has a number of Walk Sequencing Machines. Walk

Sequencing Machines are very good at dealing with standardised letters delivered in bulk from corporate utilities. They're just not so good at reading ordinary people's handwriting, that's all.

None of these mail companies has a universal delivery obligation, unlike the Royal Mail. In fact, they have no delivery obligation whatsoever. They aren't rival mail companies in a free market, as the propaganda would have you believe. None of them deliver mail at all. All they do is ride on the back of the system created and developed by the Royal Mail over several hundred years, and extract profit from it.

The process is called "downstream access". Downstream access means that private mail companies have access to any point in the Royal Mail delivery network that will yield a profit, after which it will leave the poor old postman to actually carry it to your door.

Is this what Adam Crozier told Peter Mandelson, who then repeated it on our TV screens? Not that figures are down at the delivery end of the process, but that they are down overall due to competition from private mail companies? Figures are down, but volume has stayed the same.

Then someone in the Union discovered that Royal Mail, arbitrarily, and without consultation, had reduced the estimate for the number of letters in each of those grey boxes. It had been 208. They now said it was 150.

The Union decided to double-check the figures. They ordered a manual count of the number of letters in the grey boxes in a few selected offices. Ours was one of them. Jerry volunteered to do the counting. So every morning for two weeks Jerry spent half an hour manually counting the numbers of letters in a randomly selected collection of grey boxes. He only did this for the letters, not the flats. Only one man for only two weeks, so it wasn't a rigorous scientific survey.

Nevertheless, it did give us all some idea of how much mail was actually passing through our office during that period.

On average, it seems, those boxes, which the Royal Mail claim contain only 150 letters, actually carry 267 items of mail.

I've nearly finished my story now. It is a tale of loss and deceit, of anger and despair, of the wanton destruction of an ancient and venerable organisation, much loved by everyone who uses it.

Once it is gone it will be gone for ever.

And one day, maybe, when it has passed

out of the realms of history and into myth, we will talk about it in hushed tones of reverence.

"Do you remember that? The Royal Mail? You could post a letter one day and it would be at its destination the next. There was a whole army of men and women who used to do this work. They worked day and night to get it done.

"Mail criss-crossed the country, travelling at speed. It crossed the world. There were trains and planes and vans and trucks, and huge mail centres, all carrying and sifting the mail. And still, despite the huge volumes, almost all of the mail got through.

"It handled tens of millions of letters a day, millions of packets. It was the oldest state-owned company in the world and people were proud to work for it. It did the work more efficiently than any of its rivals.

"There was a network of distinctive red pillar boxes. They stood on the corner of the street. You could post your letters into them, and they would be emptied twice a day. There were post offices in every town and every village, and when you saw a postie on the street he would smile and say good morning."

It's been 30 years since I started work for the Royal Mail: 30 years, almost to the day. I've seen a lot of changes, none of them for the better. I've seen it change its name, from Royal Mail, to Consignia, and back again. I've seen this agreement and that agreement. I've seen changes to my working practices and hours. I've suffered a huge loss of income and of status. I've seen friends and colleagues at work come and go. I've watched the atmosphere in the office go from cheerful efficiency to weariness and despair. I've seen some of my colleagues almost go out of their minds.

But what I have to say next may surprise you.

The Royal Mail is still sound. At its heart, it is still sound. The network is still sound. It still works. It is not too late to save it. It needs some money. It needs some care. It needs a return to full public ownership. It needs some accountability. It needs people to run it who care about it, who are not just running it down in order to privatise it. It needs a management who are committed to it. It needs a management with a sense of history. It is huge and unwieldy and vast and complex. It needs real attention to detail. It needs some love. It needs some time. Most of all, it needs a management who will listen to its workers and its customers at last. Its real customers. Not the corporations: Granny Smith.

There's an old lady on my round. Every year she gives me a Christmas card, and she always folds a fiver in with it.

It's always the old people. Old people are always the most generous with tips. There's a kind of old-fashioned graciousness about the way she hands it to me. She touches my hand briefly and looks me in the eye.

"For your trouble," she says, with a twinkle.

I don't open the card immediately. I save it till I get home. That's when I read the note: "For my Postman," it says. "Thank you for thinking of me every day."

That just about sums it up.

For many people the person who delivers the mail is still an important figure. We mean something. We represent birthday cards and Christmas cards, and letters from their loved ones. We represent holiday postcards and bunches of flowers and mail-order gifts from catalogues. We represent order and regularity, contact, communication, certainty in an uncertain world, routine and predictability, the ordinary round of everyday life. One thing you know – barring a strike – the postie will always be there to deliver your mail.

Granny Smith is everyone, but particularly every old lady who is alone and vulnerable, and for whom the mail service is a lifeline. I'm maybe the only person in the whole of the world who thinks about that old lady every day, even if it's only for long enough to read her name on an envelope and then to post it.

The tension here is between the Royal Mail as a profit-making business, and the Royal Mail as a public service.

It is both at the same time.

For most of the Royal Mail management — who rarely, if ever, come across the public — it represents the first; while to the delivery officer — to me, and people like me, your postman or post woman on the street, the one who brings the mail to your door — it is more than likely the second.

We had a Team Talk meeting a while back in which all of the proposed changes to the business were first being laid out. Changes in our hours and working practices. Changes to our priorities. Changes that have led to the current chaos.

We were told that the emphasis was to be on the corporate customer these days. It was what the corporations wanted that mattered. We were effectively being told that quality of service to the average customer was less important than satisfying the requirements of the corporations.

Someone piped up in the middle of it.

"What about Granny Smith?" he said. He's one of the old-fashioned sorts of postie, the kind who cares about these things.

"Granny Smith is not important," we were told. "Granny Smith doesn't matter any more."

So now you know.

"Roy Mayall" has been a postman
for a number of years.